Happy 70th Birth
I would stick to a
Reminders of all t
had in your long life
        Lots of love
              Care.
                 xxx

A real cold cat or hot pussy?

Katharine & Maurice George

MACKEREL THE TRAVELLING CAT

~ By the Sea

with numerous illustrations
by
Jennifer M Toombs

and foreword by Alan Britten

Green Dog Press

First published 2000
Published by Green Dog Press, 1 Church End, Swerford, Oxford, OX7 4AX, UK
Text © 1998, 2000 by Katharine K George and Maurice W George
Illustrations © 1999, 2000 by Jennifer M Toombs

Katharine K George and Maurice W George have asserted their rights under the Copyright, Designs and Patents Act, 1988 to be identified as the authors of this work
Jennifer M Toombs has asserted her rights under the Copyright, Designs and Patents Act, 1988 to be identified as the illustrator of this work

This book is sold subject to the condition that it shall not by way of trade or otherwise, be lent, re-sold, hired out, or otherwise circulated without the publisher's prior consent in any form of binding or cover other than that in which it is published and without a similar condition including this condition being imposed on the subsequent purchaser

All rights reserved. No part of this publication may be reproduced, stored in a retrieval system, or transmitted in any form or by any means, electronic, mechanical, photocopying, recording or otherwise, except as permitted by the UK Copyright, Designs and Patents Act 1988, without the prior permission in writing of the publisher

ISBN 0 9538143 0 0 hardback
ISBN 0 9538143 1 9 paperback

British Library Cataloguing-in-Publication Data
A CIP catalogue record for this book is available from the British Library

OTHER TITLES IN PREPARATION
MACKEREL THE TRAVELLING CAT
~ In the Hills
~ At Home

Printed in the UK by Cheney & Sons Limited, Banbury

Mackerel was an unusual cat. He gained a distinctive reputation for appearing in places and at events where people least expected a cat to be.
This book tells of his holidays in Suffolk, by the sea, in towns, villages and woodlands, and his unofficial personal adoption of the 'Aldeburgh Festival of Music and the Arts' over almost a quarter of its existence at that time.

He came to twelve consecutive festivals and became well known to many people, including those joining the regular 'Wednesday Walks'. Although he never attended any concert, he went to several art exhibitions.
Mackerel also had many other adventures, in and around his Oxfordshire home and when climbing mountains in the Lake District..... but those stories are for another time.

ACKNOWLEDGEMENTS

Many people who knew Mackerel were keen on the idea of immortalising him in print and we are grateful to all of them for their encouragement. Paul Fincham has sustained us with his initial enthusiasm and continued interest as the project evolved. Norman Scarfe who as well as appearing in the story made a critical examination of the text, pointed out the need for clarification here and there, and rightly caused us to expunge some doggerel. John Bishop also commented most helpfully on details in the text and gave us useful advice on the book's production.

Anne Deere and her dog Ace spent a few days with us one summer and a delightful memento of that occasion is her photograph of Mackerel among the flowers on one of the islands on the Meare; we are also grateful to Elizabeth Rowe for her unobserved (by us) photograph of him at the authors' feet in the coach during an excursion one Wednesday.

Our friends at Aldeburgh Productions have followed progress with interest and we particularly thank Régis Cochefert for his keen support and practical advice.

Some readers may sense a similarity of layout to those classic animal stories of Ernest Thompson Seton. Like other authors we also found them to be an inspiring model.

CONTENTS

    FOREWORD 1
1. SUFFOLK AND THE SEA 3
2. A SNAKE IN THE GRASS 11
3. WEDNESDAY WALKS 17
4. THE MEARE 25
5. "HE BITE!" 29
6. IN TOWN 35
7. BACK ON GUARD 41

FOREWORD

Anyone who went on the Aldeburgh Festival walks in the late 80's or early 90's will remember Mackerel. Most people are used to walking with dogs. To those unenlightened souls who are not cat lovers by instinct, the presence of Mackerel was initially disconcerting, then amazing, and finally uplifting. We came to look for Mackerel, and we were never disappointed. He lent to those walks a sense of the unexpected, just as the music stretches our ears beyond the merely conventional.

Yellow Horned Poppy

This book is a testament to his memory. It will delight cat lovers. It will evoke the warmest memories of Aldeburgh and Orford and Blythburgh and Tunstall, and the pleasures of so many Aldeburgh Festivals. It will also catch the imagination of anyone who likes a tale of the endearingly bizarre.

In a typically warm and generous gesture, Katharine and Maurice George have chosen to donate all their profits from the sale of this book to Aldeburgh Productions*. Those of us who love Aldeburgh are sincerely grateful. Readers, whether or not they know Suffolk, will be equally grateful for this charming chronicle of the exploits of a Most Unusual Personage.

Alan Britten is Chairman of the English Tourism Council. He is also President of the Friends of Aldeburgh Productions, a member of the Council of the University of East Anglia, President of the Queen Elizabeth Scholarship Trust and a non-executive director of Mobil Oil Company Ltd. His uncle was the composer, Benjamin Britten.

---

*Registered Charity No. 261383

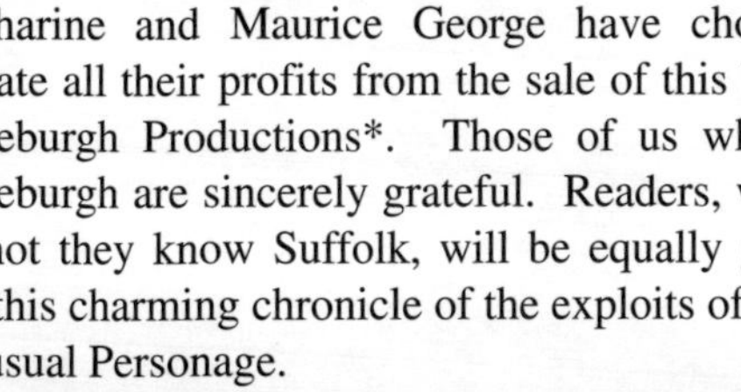

Sea Pea
(Lathyrus maritimus)

MACKEREL THE TRAVELLING CAT ~ BY THE SEA

1. SUFFOLK AND THE SEA

In July 1983 Mackerel was collected as a kitten, only a few weeks old, from a cat rescue centre. He grew up in his home in the middle of England, in the Oxfordshire countryside bordering the Cotswolds. He was a tabby cat with white socks, a smart white shirtfront and a distinctive mark on his nose. He became an adventurous animal and fond of individuals (those whom he could trust) rather than places. When away from home he was happy with a harness and lead and was an exceedingly good car traveller.

Mackerel never needed a cat basket, even when visiting his vet. He would always, either lie on the front passenger's lap or, when he was alone with the driver, on the front passenger seat. He would never interfere with the driver or wander around in the car, although he would often be interested in what was going on, especially when arriving at places he would recognise.

When he was on holiday, the car was both his travelling home and safe haven on the occasions when he was not allowed to be taken into public places. He was never left on his own other than in the car and it was there where he always took his meals. All his personal needs were attended to as his diet was simple and regular. When taken for his walks every morning and evening, he would make good use of *convenient* molehills.

After nine months of growing up and various day excursions from home for training, Mackerel was then introduced to hotel life with a spring

holiday among the high hills and mountains of the Lake District in the north-west of England. By then, fully accustomed to his harness and lead, he climbed intrepidly over two well-known peaks. It was thus as an experienced traveller and walker that in June 1984 he came to Suffolk on the east coast, during the 37th Aldeburgh Festival, and saw the sea for the first time.

Cats often like to assert their independence and on being carried to the car for departure he would always protest vocally at being taken away from his regular haunts. Very soon though, he came to realise that the disturbance to his routine meant that there was going to be a holiday. He would give himself away by never refusing to have his harness put on – the appearance of that and his lead was an infallible sign to him that he would be going on a journey. Furthermore he soon came to know what all those suitcases meant, and the turmoil of packing, which gave him plenty of warning and the opportunity for him to slip away and 'take to the hills'. Thus it was we knew that he clearly preferred to be with us rather than be left behind at home.

When Mackerel first came to Suffolk his family base for the Aldeburgh Festival was in the village of Orford at the Crown & Castle hotel, across the lane from a magnificent mediaeval castle. Orford is only a few minutes drive through the woods from the Snape Maltings Concert Hall, where, during festival time, most of the principal musical events are held. Orford's lofty church, although but a remnant of a much larger building, has also heard much fine music including the first performances of Benjamin Britten's *Church Parables* and some festival concerts still take place there.

Orford is an inland village, on the river Ore – an extension of the Alde which once flowed into the sea at Aldeburgh. Now, blocked by a natural bank of shingle stones, the river turns abruptly southwards, only a few yards from the sea. It changes its name to Ore and flows fourteen miles behind the great shingle bank of Orford Beach before it reaches the sea. The shingle bank has steadily built up and extended southward from Aldeburgh over the centuries; at the time when the great castle was built by Henry II at Orford, the village was an important seaport.

The grounds surrounding the castle were once within the castle bailey, and there are mounds and ridges where the now vanished walls and outbuildings had once been. The grounds and nearby footpaths provided excellent walking territory for Mackerel, with plenty of rabbits causing additional excitement.

During the day, explorations soon extended to the network of footpaths in the neighbourhood. The river bank, fields and local lanes provided a varied menu of interesting adventures and none more so than one day by the river Ore when he came face to face (allowing for the difference in altitude) with a bullock. Whether it was Mackerel's familiarity with the species when on his own, crossing the water meadow near his home, or that he was giving a fine display of *lofty* indifference we shall never know, but the bullock was certainly amazed.

The narrow path on top of the raised river bank with its fringe of long grass, and the field footpaths, with tall grass and crops, made good cat country, with excellent cover giving him a feeling of security which was absent in the more open spaces. With such assurance that danger was not immediate, Mackerel would often make the pace, running on ahead to the full length of his long extending lead. The kinds of bird present on the river and adjacent marshes, very different from those in his surroundings at home, were avocets and oystercatchers, reed warblers and buntings. However, Mackerel seemed to acknowledge them all with the same degree of resignation he usually accorded to any wild life he could not chase when on holiday.

Walks in the late evening would usually be around the keep, which is all that remains of the castle buildings. A flight of ancient stone steps hugs the wall, leading up to the heavy iron-studded door. Standing at the top of the steps it can be appreciated, from the extent of the view, why the castle had been built there.

Nearby, at the edge of the village, we would watch a gardener tending his vegetables and on the edge of the allotments there was a row of rabbit hutches; we could see the occupants comfortably sleeping or munching. Further out, the river could be seen but as the details of the marshes and

SUFFOLK AND THE SEA

meadows faded into the dusk, the sound of birdcalls became the only sign of activity. In the distance ships passed to and from Harwich and Felixstowe, and the flashes from the lightships marking their way would indicate the horizon we could no longer see. Often there would be mist out to sea, and the sad, low warning sound of the fog-horn of the Orford Ness lighthouse would always remind us of Britten's opera *Peter Grimes*.

Mackerel would at first stare at the distant view but then pay more attention to the surrounding trees and bushes, his cat's eyes seeing in the shadows what was denied to human sight.

It was a ritual late at night to try the door of the castle and, if it did not open, strike it solemnly three times. But it never opened and no-one ever answered our 'Knocking on the moonlit door.' If they had, no-one would have been more scared than we. Perhaps if Mackerel had been a *black* cat we might have had more success?

Mackerel's meals were an unvarying routine. He was fed once a day in the early evening, and always in the car. At festival time, he usually had his supper while his master and mistress were having their meal, which was often at Mrs Pinney's fish restaurant, the Butley Orford Oysterage, overlooking the village square. Some years later he had the honour to be introduced to Mrs Pinney outside her restaurant. As always his behaviour was impeccable and he did not receive or expect any tit-bit.

The Snape Maltings Concert Hall is alongside the river Alde, with reed beds and tidal mudflats to the east, fields to the south, and footpaths leading into the countryside and along the river banks. Behind the concert hall are places for parking cars, including some in good shade under a double row of pink-flowering horse-chestnut trees. The friendly attendants soon recognised the cat rather than the driver, and would direct the car to the shady spots. He would be given a chance to have a quick pee if required among the soft leaves and long grass nearby. He would then settle down for the evening, often on the back parcel shelf. This gave him a good view of horses in a neighbouring field and nearby hedges and undergrowth where there were always birds foraging.

The general bustle of people, a few seeing to their dogs, more arriving in cars, some having picnics, would mysteriously and suddenly disappear and all would be peaceful during the progress of the concert. In the quietness Mackerel would give himself a wash and certainly have a cat-nap. Much later, most of the cars would equally suddenly start to come to life, disperse in their separate ways into the night and leave the place at peace once again.

Having had a chat with friends over coffee in the old restaurant, his master and mistress would return; we would always be greeted with a yawn, a stretch, purrs and excited successions of *meows*.

SUFFOLK AND THE SEA

Back at home in Oxfordshire, almost the farthest possible from the sea, the drive and garage yard had years ago been laid down with beach shingle. For amusement Mackerel would suddenly go mad and attack an inoffensive smooth pebble, whirling round with all four feet seemingly perched on it. Perhaps the sea-shore at Aldeburgh – pure shingle and known for its great variety of pebbles of many different colours and occasional amber – might have given him endless fun and even some recollection of home? But no, the sea beyond and its immensity seemed too much for his brain to comprehend.

He was not frightened of the sea, he simply did not like it, contrary to Orlando of literary fame. Nevertheless, he did not mind looking at the same view which Orlando would have seen from the top of the town steps, recalling Kathleen Hale's illustration in her book *A Seaside Holiday*, for which Aldeburgh was the model. Best of all he liked to curl up and sun-bathe on a blanket spread out on the shingle, with a windbreak set up to protect against the breezes, and to remain there until the sun began to sink towards the landward horizon.

Although small and inconspicuous, especially in crowds, Mackerel was adept at avoiding being trampled on. He comfortably attended many art exhibitions and craft or antique fairs without being much noticed; when people see someone with a

lead they automatically think that a dog is at the other end of it and generally there would be no reason for them to look further.

The Peter Pears Gallery, part of what was once the antiquated Suffolk Hotel in Aldeburgh High Street, is on an upper floor and is reached by visitors from the old coach-way outside, via an all-metal open stairway. The first time Mackerel was taken there he had never seen or been on metal stairs before; he disliked the ringing sound it made when people stepped on it, so he always needed to be carried up to the gallery – but once there, he was happy. Wherever he was taken, he would never be bored or demand to leave – even from exhibitions of the most unintelligible kind.

He used to pay an annual visit to the Aldringham craft market, which is in the country, a couple of miles northwest of Aldeburgh. He was always made welcome, even though he would have to be stopped from sometimes trying to examine the contents of some of the lower shelves. The main room has a flight of open stairs to an upper floor. They are fine, smooth wood and quiet. He enjoyed going up and down them and looking down through the balustrading at the floor below.

2. A SNAKE IN THE GRASS

When we stayed at the Crown & Castle at Orford with Mackerel it was always at the far end of a row of 'chalets' built down one side of the hotel garden. The front door opened onto the parking area for visitors' cars, but the back door was onto a small private verandah facing the garden and afternoon sunshine. This was ideal for the cat and after the first stay, when we arrived the following year, he knew which was 'his' chalet. After being booked in at the reception in the hotel, he knew which door to stop at, and nipped in as soon as it was unlocked and opened.

The Crown & Castle, although much altered over the years, was an old building. Beyond the main garden of the hotel lay an area of long grass and weeds, which we were surprised to find, after further enquiry, had been a bowling green. It was a telling example of how the best kept green-sward can change into jungle when left to itself. However, it served as a useful out-of-the-way spot for Mackerel's needs, additionally providing an involuntary early morning bath when wet with dew.

The hotel cat was, coincidentally, called Kipper, a little timid one so the birds in the garden were neither bothered with her, nor with Mackerel – unlike the alert sparky ones at home. While our cat lazed on the threshold in the sunshine, the birds would happily peck and dustbath in the flowerbed nearby. They seemed to lead an equally lazy life; one young thrush particularly appeared to be the epitome of somnolent birditude.

After a while we decided to rent a cottage within easy reach of Snape for our annual fortnight's holiday. This we did for a number of years and it was interesting to see how Mackerel would quickly adapt himself, getting to know what was and what was not allowed.

Staying in a strange home can bring unexpected adventures. The owner of one holiday cottage had a pond in the garden which required continual topping up, using a translucent, green, cross-braided hosepipe which was laid from an outside tap through long grass. The first time Mackerel saw the pipe, gleaming in the sunshine, he instantly became strangely and exceedingly wary. He gave an abrupt, backward leap and crouched down staring at it intently, as if it were a sleeping snake which at any moment would wake up and attack him. Only after we had handled it and shown him that it was thoroughly 'dead' did he eventually go over it, and then still only with a quick, energetic spring.

After two or three experiences of having to pack hurriedly on a Saturday morning and move from the holiday cottage, leaving it spick and span, and booking into a hotel for the remainder of the weekend, all between changing into appropriate clothing, going to a recital in one place and a concert somewhere else, we at last decided that we would go back to staying in one spot for the whole holiday.

By then we had stayed with Mackerel in Aldeburgh for short visits at two hotels on the sea front but neither had 'chalets', which we found for all of us to be the best arrangement for independence and relaxation. It was then we discovered that Uplands Hotel, opposite Aldeburgh parish church, had three groups of chalets in its extensive and beautiful garden. The hotel was run by the Tidder family and we soon found that everything there was much to our liking and over the years the end chalet became our 'home from home'.

Uplands is another hotel within the fabric of an old house, this time with notable associations. It was the home of Elizabeth Garrett Anderson, an early woman medical practitioner and as mayor of Aldeburgh the first woman to hold this office in England. The Garrett family were also great pioneer industrialists and are commemorated in a museum created in part of their former factory in nearby Leiston.

When we first stayed at Uplands, there was no other animal there, but one day during Mackerel's second visit we found Bob Tidder and his daughter trying to coax a stray black kitten from under their garden shed. Eventually they succeeded in winning her confidence and thus Mittens entered into the life of the hotel and was in residence for the remainder of Mackerel's visits.

Cats are naturally territorial animals, so touring away from home demands special behaviour when

meeting any resident cat. Mackerel generally took the view that his interests were best served if he assumed an aloof attitude, so from the beginning he would assert his position and therefore relations were usually cool between himself and any resident cat. Antagonistic confrontations with Mittens were consequently not encouraged and Mackerel was always told that it was the height of bad manners for a guest to swear at a resident. Curiously, although the church-yard was where he took his regular morning walks, he never met the local cat king, the ginger and white Samson.

Mackerel's holidays in June coincided with moulting time and, although his fur was short, casting of his hair around cottage or hotel, or in the car, was to be avoided. Brushing regularly helped but was not the complete answer. So why not get him professionally groomed? Consulting the 'Yellow Pages' business directory did not list anything for cats but one small but enterprising kennels was willing to help. Since the crazy idea was mine alone, I took responsibility for the enterprise and Mackerel to the kennels, while Maurice took a walk along the sea edge with feelings of dire foreboding.

On arrival and getting out of the car, the cat and I were assailed by a chorus of barks, yaps and yowls coming from behind a low building. Mackerel clearly wanted to go back into the car. With him tucked under my left arm I went into the building and introduced ourselves to a pleasant woman. I reiterated what I had told her over the telephone and at the same time being very conscious of the prevalent dog atmosphere – as a stranger might feel if gatecrashing into an exclusive club.

"That's fine," said she, "I've never been asked to do a cat before, but it's very straightforward, and he looks a fine fellow. How long did it take to train him ...?"

By the time I had answered all the questions which were usually asked about this unusual cat, Mackerel had got used to the back-ground dog music; however, worse was to come.

"I always do the grooming in that far building, through the dog compound where I have my sealyhams," she said as I followed her outside. "Sealyhams are my speciality. . Have you a cat basket?"

I explained that Mackerel's only basket was a cat basket in the same manner as a dog has a dog basket, in other words his basket was back at home in the side passage alongside his drinking bowl. He had never been in a closed basket apart from the time when we had collected him as a kitten, and he did not need a closed basket any more than a dog does, but of course I would carry him, and he would clearly let me know if he objected.

Holding him rather more firmly under my arm I found myself a few moments later feeling like a boat being launched into dangerous waters. My guide opened the wire gate into the compound, we went through and she shut it behind me. We then literally waded through what seemed to be a

Field-poppy

churning sea of sealyhams; I kept up a continual, calm explanation to Mackerel that it was perfectly all right, that there was nothing to worry about. I felt him stiffen and if a dog jumped a bit too close, he took no chances and spat with fury.

Having reached shore in the shape of a table-top within the far building, Mackerel disembarked from under my arm and the professional grooming commenced. He tolerated it, even the fine wire brush. When it was over, we retraced our steps without mishap, paid our bill with exchange of compliments, returned to the car and drove back to base.

Maurice was relieved to see the cat still in one piece, both physically and mentally. After a few days I admitted that the experiment was not worth repeating.

3. WEDNESDAY WALKS

During each week of the Aldeburgh Festival fortnight in June, one day – usually the Wednesday – has been, for many years, traditionally devoted to a whole day's excursion in and around Suffolk. These are popular and up to two hundred people take part. Coaches take the walkers to the starting point and there is often a walk of two or three miles to some place of interest. Each coachload forms a separate group led by a local person familiar with the area. Seen from a distance the groups are a strange sight when strung out over fields or marshes or along the top of a coastal ridge.

Sometimes part or all of the walking might be in a town, with stops for sightseeing. Country houses, castles, archæological sites, farms and gardens are reached across fields, marshes and beaches in weather ranging from blazing sun to wind and rain. Mackerel came on the coach and went on more than a dozen such festival walks, where he became a familiar sight in all weathers.

At the end of the morning walk all gather at a suitable picnic place and are provided with packed lunches; ideally these are consumed in the sunshine with the party perhaps spread around the lawns of a big house. But, while a walk can be planned, the same cannot be said for the weather so shelter must always be at hand if needed. Village halls are generally comfortable but sitting on hay bales in an open sided barn on a wet, windy day shows how well we can all make do if there is no better alternative.

No matter where the picnics took place, Mackerel always behaved impeccably, patiently settling down and taking no notice, with everyone around him eating and drinking and crackling paper lunch-bags and napkins.

Following the picnic, there is always a further walk, with a new objective, after which everyone rejoins the coaches to be taken back to Aldeburgh.

There were just two occasions when Mackerel was frightened, and both times it was the result of a sudden unexpected noise in, for him, a totally unrelated context. A coach, like a car, seemed to him to be a safe haven, until the first time the driver released the air brakes with a loud *hiss-s-s*. Mackerel's sense of security was suddenly shattered, perhaps because he had a primæval anticipation of being attacked by giant tigers. As these did not materialise he soon became used to the journeys and would sit quietly at our feet.

The other occasion was during a visit to a large house, when an excellent talk was given indoors to all of us. At the end of the talk we naturally all applauded, clapping our hands enthusiastically and creating a sudden torrent of noise which must have sounded as if the North Sea itself was bursting in through the windows. Without a firm hold and quiet reassurances that all was well, Mackerel would have taken flight more swiftly than the imagined sea-gulls coming in with the tide. When nothing else alarming followed he regained his

WEDNESDAY WALKS

poise; having heard clapping hands once, the sound of it never disturbed him again.

In the early days it was thought best to travel with a rucksack into which he would creep when he did not want to walk, but later he would prefer to ride like a furry scarf, or on one shoulder resting his front paws on the back of his carrier's hand.

Hot sun for a long time and with no shelter was troublesome. A paper hat with holes for his ears was tried, reminiscent of cart horses in Brittany. It was some help but a more permanent and reliable method was necessary.

One particularly warm day we were paying one of our regular visits to the pleasant and interesting town of Southwold, on the coast, about twelve miles north of Aldeburgh. It is distinguished for many things, from its colourful, homely beach huts, the lighthouse, the brewery with its beautiful white dray horses, to its curious little triangular 'greens' here and there in the town. Passing a corner shop we saw a paper sun-shade which prompted an idea for shielding the cat. The sun-shade was bought and experiments began. It was soon found that, when opened, it was too easily caught by the wind making it very difficult to hold it firmly. Eventually, using an office punch, we pierced the shade with a large number of holes to allow a draught of air through. So he would ride on a left shoulder with the sunshade grasped in the left hand and held over him. This was still awkward, but effective.

Mackerel helped to keep himself cool by readily panting and his paws would sweat, his pads leaving little damp footprints on any smooth surface he walked across. He could always refresh himself if necessary from water offered in the palm of a hand, but this was seldom needed and even after a long day his liquid intake seemed little more than usual.

The rain was no bother; on several occasions he got very wet, as he did many times during his visits to the Lake District. Indeed, on his independent walks at home, it seemed that he would go out in stormy weather to get thoroughly wet as a good excuse to be rubbed down with his towel when he got back.

Once he joined the group waiting for the first coach outside the Moot Hall in Aldeburgh, when the rain was already pouring down. Invisible to them, his old friends said that obviously we had left him behind.

"...Not surprising, weather like this will never clear up..."

But a partly unzipped fastening to a hefty mountain type anorak revealed his little head peeking out. One excursion walk ended in Ufford church where, one after another, to the dismay of the parson, some very wet walkers dripped their way into the church and added to the growing pool of water on the floor. However, thanks to being tucked inside a capacious anorak, Mackerel was kept tolerably dry.

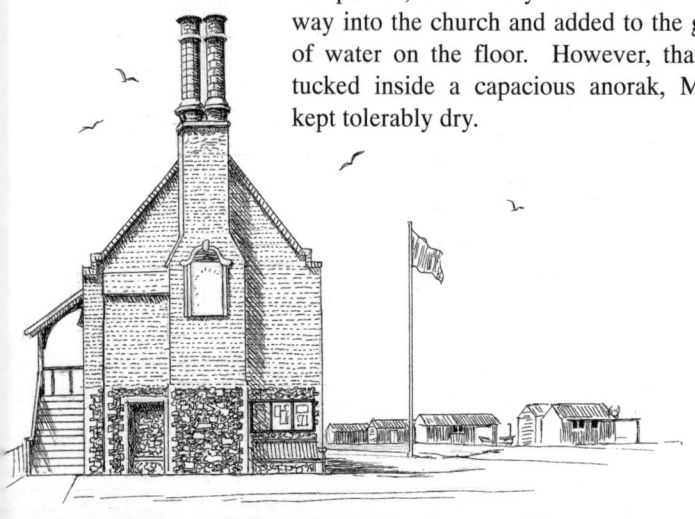

WEDNESDAY WALKS

On another particularly wet occasion we were all kindly invited by the owners of a large country house we were visiting, to shelter from the rain and have our picnic lunches indoors, seated on the floor in one of the big rooms. Having first discarded all our muddy boots and shoes in the great stone-flagged entrance hall, all of us settled down. One sensitive visitor's imagination had already been struck by the sight of two gigantic oil paintings hung on either side of the hall which depicted, in over life-sized and bloodthirsty detail, game of various kinds being rent apart by hounds. When she saw what she thought was the house-cat apparently harnessed into a corner, she was convinced that some terrible dark deeds of cruelty were being inflicted in real life. Fortunately Mackerel was easily able to prove that he was in fact a visitor and very comfortable, thanks.

For his part, Mackerel was unmoved by visual art with one slight exception. This was fleetingly when he was first shown the memorial to two local doctors, Robin and Nora Acheson, which is by the model-boat pond near the Moot Hall. It is a beautiful bronze sculpture of their pet dog. Mackerel momentarily pricked his ears and sniffed – but that was all.

A walk across the fields once ended spectacularly with a rapid descent into an old chalk-pit, which had been made into an enchanting, secluded garden by the owner who dwelt in a nearby cottage. The garden was filled with seemingly every kind of old-fashioned rose, and the romantic feel of the place was heightened by there being a cave in the cliff occupied by a protected bat colony. The sudden change from field path to apparent mountainside did not trouble Mackerel, who was by then well experienced in ascending and descending rocky places during his visits to the Cumbrian hills.

The planning of many of the excursions, including those during the time of Mackerel's visits, made extensive use of the knowledge and experience of Norman Scarfe, the writer and historian. At various points during the outings, Norman would talk to the groups about all kinds of interesting historical and architectural matters concerning the buildings and surrounding countryside.

When inside a church, Norman would often speak from the pulpit to the temporary congregation of walkers, to elaborate on the finer points of interest. While this was going on Mackerel would agree not to pull on his lead by trying to explore the darker recesses of the building. This restraint was not always imposed during family visits, as for example when he was allowed to climb to the top of the rood stair of East Mersea church in Essex.

When talking to us outside, Norman's vantage point might be a grassy knoll or up a few garden steps. Despite sunshine, flowers and birdsong, Mackerel would ignore these sights and sounds of nature, which would otherwise hold his interest; he would appear to listen attentively, and he certainly never made any comments.

MACKEREL THE TRAVELLING CAT ~ BY THE SEA

4. THE MEARE

A mile up the coast from Aldeburgh is the village of Thorpeness. It was originally a hamlet given over to fishing and, according to some, smuggling. In 1908 Stuart Ogilvie became the owner of the Sizewell estate and over the next twenty-five years he created a holiday village around the cluster of a few old houses and an ancient inn. He gave it buildings which he felt that no self-respecting East Anglian village should be without, such as a church, a public hall and a windmill. Piped water, however, was a necessity for the potential market of holidaying townsfolk, and to avoid the blot of an ugly conventional water tower, he built the famous 'House in the Clouds' to conceal a 30,000-gallon-tank. To provide leisurely amusement, an adjacent tidal fen was enclosed, dug out and turned into a shallow boating lake and given a local name, but with rustic spelling, *Meare*. A variety of boats were supplied for hire, many of which are still in use after eighty or more years.

The Meare was provided with an archipelago of romantic islands, some of which were furnished with fairy-tale and other discreet 'eye-catchers' for children. Some of these have to be passed by with the utmost stealth, such as *The Pirates' Lair* and, half hidden by yellow irises, *The Crocodile*. *The Fort* with mock cannons still guards the south shore near the islands. *Safe* passages can be made either along the peaceable north shore, bordered by a golf course, clumps of yellow lupins, and gardens, with the windmill and the House in the Clouds behind, or across the open water directly from the boat landings with nothing more fearsome than likely encounters with the many birds inhabiting the Meare.

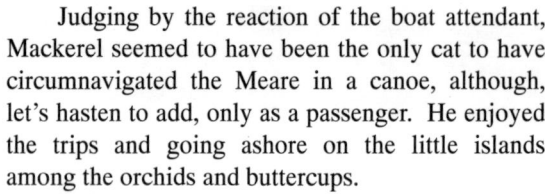

Judging by the reaction of the boat attendant, Mackerel seemed to have been the only cat to have circumnavigated the Meare in a canoe, although, let's hasten to add, only as a passenger. He enjoyed the trips and going ashore on the little islands among the orchids and buttercups.

Naturally he was interested in the bird life but even the swans didn't take any notice of him – perhaps they could not believe their eyes. He used to watch the grebes diving and swimming out of sight to emerge again some distance away, also the coots and ducks. And perhaps the swallows swooping down low over the boat would remind him of his unpopularity with the house martins at home.

Near the Meare is a cafe with tables and chairs outside. It is a favourite spot for visitors, who are usually joined by the local sparrows and ducks looking for crumbs. When on a lead Mackerel seemed to hold his hunting instincts in check, so he tolerated the sparrows and was not known to hiss at the ducks. Just inside the entrance to the cafe there was a notice: *'NO DOGS ALLOWED BEYOND THIS POINT'*. As if to make sure this edict was obeyed, there was an old parrot in a nearby cage who, whenever he saw the cat, would squawk with indignant fury.

THE MEARE

A good way to propel a boat on the Meare is using Hiawatha's time-honoured method. It can just be done, although the design of our 'canoes' are not at all like his. You board one of the old, narrow, clinker-built boats and sit high up *on* the extreme stern. You use one single-blade paddle on one side only, as far back as is comfortably possible. Suppose you chose to use the paddle on your left side, then to keep the boat moving straight ahead you turn the blade slightly anti-clockwise at the end of each stroke. To move to starboard you don't twist the blade, and to move to port you backstroke. The beauty of this method is that you are facing the way you are travelling, you control both steering and moving forward, and it is extremely leisurely. It is neither as energetic nor as wet-making as using double paddles.

If there is a second person in the boat they can sit for'ard and relax and occasionally paddle, as required, on the opposite side. This is useful when a storm is brewing and you want to get back to the boat-landing quickly. The other advantage is that when you have an animal on board, the whole of the boat is in front of you and you can watch what he is getting up to.

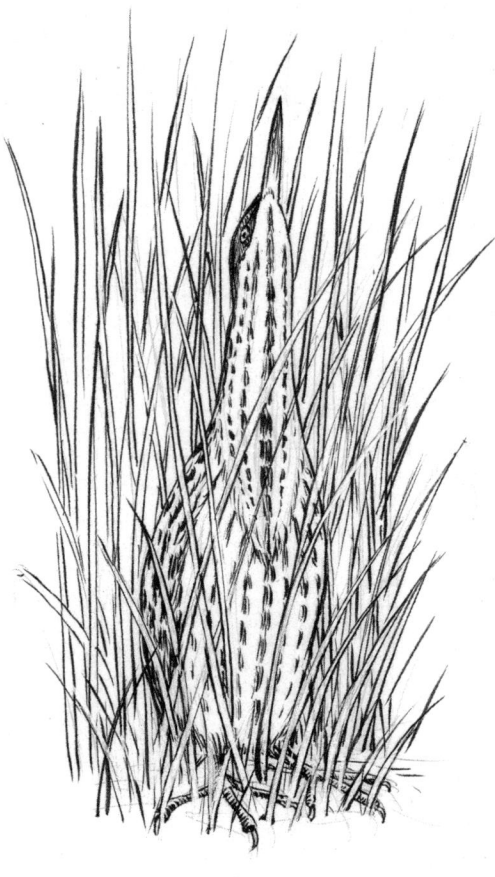

Bittern 'freezing'

5. "HE BITE!"

Blackheath Mansion, as it was then known, is a large house with extensive woodland and a garden which borders the north bank of the River Alde at its broadest point on the tidal reach between Aldeburgh and Snape. Receptions for Friends of the Aldeburgh Festival were often held there. Mackerel came to several of these, where he made discreet accompanied explorations of the gardens. While everyone else admired the flowers and trees, Mackerel liked to examine the rabbit holes and long grass.

One special Friends event we went on was an organised visit to Notcutts Nurseries near Woodbridge, where the party, and Mackerel, who listened with solemn interest, were welcomed by Charles Notcutt, the proprietor and eminent horticulturalist. We were treated to demonstrations of various grafting techniques among acres of flourishing rose-cuttings and a tour of hot and humid propagation houses. For Mackerel, this was merely a series of exotic and unusual gardens. Such extremes of environment did not seem to bother him and he watched attentively while each aspect of the work of the nursery was described.

At less interesting stopping places, for cats that is, Mackerel would just take a nap. However, picnics in the woods were quite different. There would be more birds and insects to enliven the scene and shadows in which all manner of things might be happening. Then, after we had eaten, there would be a walk with bracken and undergrowth to explore and fallen timber on which to sharpen his claws.

Pub gardens were a favourite haunt. There were always new sights and new smells which would entertain him when he was not sitting quietly under the table snoozing or washing himself. The first time he was taken into the village inn at Middleton the publican looked over the bar to see Mackerel. His wife was preparing food in the next room.

"There's a cat out here," he called out to her teasingly. "He's on the end of a string, and he *bite*!"

She hurriedly came into the bar and looked worried until she realised why everyone was laughing!

Mackerel visited many churches and the routine became well established. Entering the churchyard he would often lead the way to the church door and once inside would conduct a silent patrol as far as the extent of his lead would allow. It was not his custom to climb on to the benches but steps and stairs were a constant attraction. Whatever were his thoughts about church architecture, he did not comment aloud and other visitors would not be aware of his presence until they saw him. On leaving the church he would go round the outside of the building and examine a few headstones; then we would say "Back to the car" and he would retrace his steps to where we were parked.

"HE BITE!"

Mackerel would always be taken for a last walk before bedtime, the nearest he would get to a night hunt while on holiday. Around dusk a good place for these walks was Tunstall Common. This was especially interesting because it was also the haunt of nightjars, mysterious summer visitors who fly at dusk trapping moths in their whiskered beaks for their evening supper. From their perches on the surrounding pine trees they emit a remarkable churring sound, and when they fly, if you are lucky and they are close enough, you may hear their wings *clapping* – an unusual noise which they make during their display flights. Sometimes, close to the ground, among grass and heather, tiny dots of the palest green light from glow-worms would be seen.

Mackerel took no notice of any of this despite there being no nightjars or glow-worms at home.

Early one fine, warm evening we decided that, with luck, the nightjars would soon be getting busy, so Tunstall Common was just the place to go to. When we arrived, as usual we backed the car well off the road and at right-angles to it. Behind the car a sandy track led off into pine woodland and the common. The track was barred to vehicles by a long tree-trunk, each end secured to a post with a chain and padlock. Mackerel knew the spot well, and was soon taking us along the track to his favourite rounds, the various bushes, soft sand, pine-cones to chase, and hunting grounds for moths and daddy-long-legs.

After a while something made us look back, and there in the distance we could see another car had arrived and parked by ours. But we could not see it very clearly, because it was on the roadside and instead of being parked alongside our car, it was parked across it, so that on our return it would be impossible for us to drive away. We decided to find out what was going on.

"Come on, Mackerel, back to the car. Quick, quick!"

He understood far more words and phrases of ours than we understood of his, convincing him of his greater intelligence.

As we got nearer, we saw that it was a police car. Nearer still we could see a police officer sitting quietly at the wheel. We stood by the driver's door and he wound down the window. He looked at us both, placidly but intently.

"Mr George?" he said at last.

"Why, yes!"

"Of such-and-such address?"

Somewhat surprised at the accuracy, and thinking apprehensively, *bad news from home?* except there was not that kind of air about him –

"Yes."

"May I ask you what you are doing here?"

"Taking our cat for a walk."

"All the way from Oxfordshire!?"

..... No doubt somewhere in the files at Woodbridge police station – which happens to be opposite Buttrum's windmill which Mackerel once visited – there is a dry report carefully recording

"HE BITE!"

that on a particular day in June (time and date noted) a certain vehicle (registration number also entered) was found, apparently abandoned, and that from details radioed to HQ the owner's name and address was traced – but no, the vehicle had been neither abandoned nor stolen. Two persons had emerged from the common and were satisfactorily identified as the lawful owner and his wife. Evidence of their explanation for being there was seen at the site in question, all four furry legs of it and with a furry tail.

It is to be hoped that the officer won a pint or two from his pals with his story and for being on the cat-watch.

Angel, Blythburgh Church

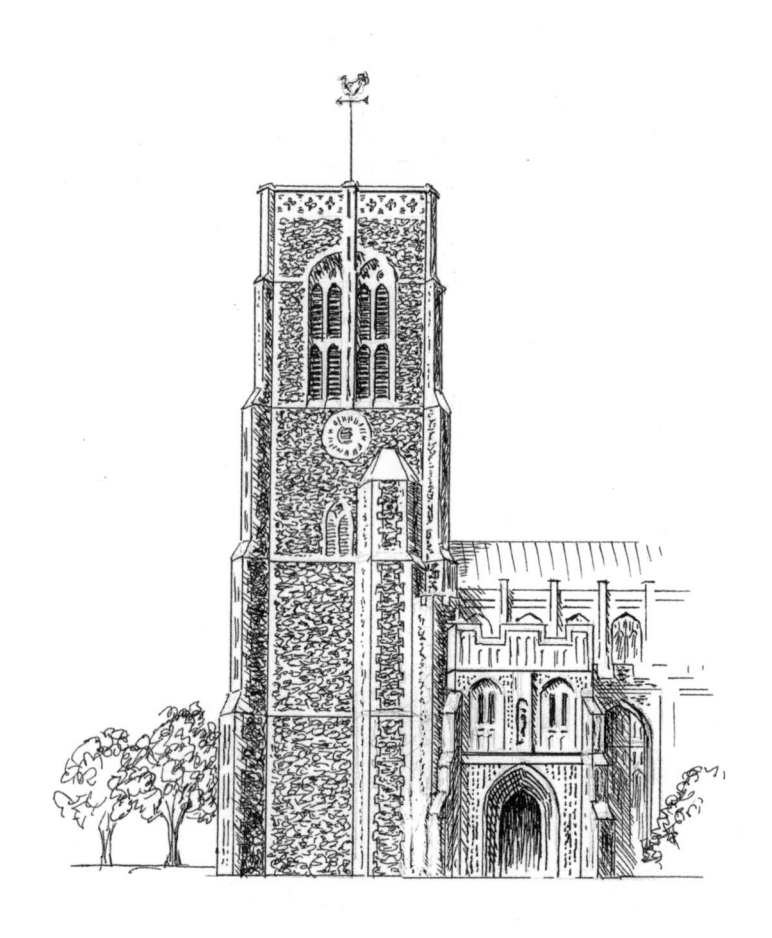

Southwold Church

6. IN TOWN

In towns or villages Mackerel clearly preferred being indoors; if any door was pushed open he would cheerfully enter and take immediate interest in his surroundings, and would never have to be carried, whether in churches, shops or the hairdressers. He was a connoisseur of bookshops, where he would patiently move from one set of shelves to another and avoid the occasional unsuspecting human feet.

In all of the several bookshops we visited regularly, he would be welcomed and then taken for granted, because he was so well behaved. In one bookshop however, we would hide his presence from the proprietor for as long as possible while we hurriedly scanned the shelves. This was not on account of any antipathy on the part of the bookseller with the imminent risk of being cast out of the shop. On the contrary! Once Mackerel had been spotted, there followed a prolonged performance of cat worship and a seemingly endless interrogation about him and his ways, all of which was anathema to an effective book-browse.

The proprietor, a sturdy man, would call him a "pretty puddy-tat" and emphatically argue that he was a "lady cat". He confidently assured us that he always knew in an instant the sex of any cat.

"No, no," he would tell 'her'. "At your size and with that boo'ful face you're not a little Tommy, are you? No, of course not!"

Telling him Mackerel's medical history never seemed to penetrate, and we desisted from subjecting our cat to a public indignity simply for the sake of pursuing a futile argument. For all that, the cat-loving bookman was always kind and friendly, and now he is sadly missed; he and his Southwold bookshop are no more.

One day, again in Southwold, Mackerel was riding shoulder-high when a woman came running up. Then she realised her unhappy mistake. She thought we had found her own cat, which had wandered off during their weekend visit and was still not about when the time came for them to leave for home. Except when Mackerel was on his own in the car, or sometimes when in our room, he was always kept on his lead when on holiday, so that he could not add to the numbers of stray cats. His harness had a brass tag attached with simply VET and his vets' telephone number engraved on both sides.

However, there was once a time when we might have had to telephone his vets to alert them for telephone messages. Mackerel was always frightened and would run out of the way if whoever was holding his lead should stumble. Fortunately this very seldom happened, but one day it did. We were in Woodbridge, which is an old market town twelve miles from Aldeburgh on the estuary of the river Deben. We were there for the

IN TOWN

day to explore the town with its many interesting buildings.

In the afternoon, we were returning to our coach having visited Buttrum's windmill (opposite the Woodbridge police station). Mackerel was walking ahead along a narrow street in the middle of the town, when suddenly he heard behind him the sounds of an abrupt running trip and a fall. He immediately sprang aside, but his lead had been dropped. He bolted across the street, at the time fortunately free of traffic, and through an open doorway, into what happened to be a dignified estate agents. It was a large, neat room with several desks, behind each of which people were quietly working. Undaunted, the cat hurtled across the room, his lead flying, and shot up a flight of open stairs under the startled gaze of the staff who then saw his minder following in hot pursuit. Mackerel was duly gathered up and customary calm was restored amid the wonderment of all around.

Thereafter a loose waistband was always looped through the handle of the lead. This in the event proved to be extremely useful as it could allow both hands to be free while the lead was still secure.

To an inquisitive cat every shop offered new territory to explore. Adnams Wine & Cellar Shop at Southwold was one such place where Mackerel soon became a recognised and welcome visitor. Perhaps the wine racks with their labels with pictures of far-off lands, and the strange smell of spices, made him wonder where all these objects had come from.

Other places were Butchers the outfitters, and Joyce's the hairdressers, both in the high street at Aldeburgh. Going into the hairdressers caused great surprise but he lived up to assurances that he was well behaved; he quickly and patiently settled down under his mistress's chair, not minding the strange surroundings and occasional splash of water.

Many dogs are naturally or sometimes even trained to be antagonistic towards cats. One dark moonless night Mackerel was taken for his routine stroll and this time it was in Aldeburgh along a path which follows the shoreline near the Moot Hall. It was quite late and no-one seemed to be about when suddenly an indistinct shape in the distance could be seen approaching. Mackerel, however, did not turn a hair, even though the shape soon materialised into a black retriever. A few moments later its owner also emerged from the darkness. After he got over his surprise at seeing a cat on a lead he explained that his dog was always friendly towards cats, something that Mackerel had sensed well before the dog came near.

On the first Sunday of every festival an opening service would be held in the morning at Aldeburgh parish church, at which an eminent cleric would be invited to come and officiate. The sermon at such times would be especially interesting with a wide appeal.

Mackerel was once taken to one of these services. We arrived early so as to sit unobtrusively at the back, but an elderly gentleman was already seated at the gangway end of it, so we took the pew in front of him. After some attempts to go exploring and being quietly but firmly told to settle down, Mackerel did so, and as the church filled he was hardly noticed by those passing by us to occupy the remainder of the pew. The service proceeded uneventfully and soon we were listening to the sermon, which quickly proved to be interesting – except to one behind us. At first the sound was indistinct, but after a while it developed into a gentle, but persistent, unmistakable *snore!*

This was most embarrassing and distracting. The gentleman was evidently on his own so there was no-one next to him to give him a persuasive shove. There was nothing to be done except hope that the noise did not increase too much.

At last the service, rather marred, came to an end and everyone began to move and go their various ways. Wondering if the old gentleman needed rousing ... but no! He was as wide awake and spry as anyone. The snoring had been coming from a dog, curled up behind the back pew, sleeping peacefully until his owner in the congregation came to fetch him. While Mackerel's upbringing had partly been modelled on the way a dog can be trained, his cat personality was always treated with the greatest respect; we would never have risked leaving him on his own at the back like that. *Vive la différence!*

7. BACK ON GUARD

The room in a turmoil, packing to go home, the car gradually being filled to bursting, the polite farewells at the reception – the only occasions he was allowed across the threshold of the hotel were at arrival and on departure. Mackerel so clearly understood the meaning of all these activities.

When at last everything was ready for the off, Mackerel's own 'pussy-bag' would be strategically handy and a bottle of water placed in the passenger's door bin and perhaps a map or newspaper also handy to shield him from the sun shining through the passenger's window. The passenger would be sitting ready with the cat's knee-cloth draped to protect clothing from his moult.

"Up, up!" he would then be told.

Up he would jump onto the passenger's lap and remain there, enjoying the three or four hours' drive, with a break for *them* and an offer of a flower bed or long grass for him during the day. If the break was around six or seven in the evening, there would be his usual supper for him as well.

He always recognised the approach near home and every time would sit up with his front paws on the windscreen ledge. On arrival the routine was for him to be placed on the ledge, where he had to remain while the passenger got out of the car to open the drive gate for the car to be driven through. We would stop in the yard and, still kept on his lead, he would go ahead to the front door, wait while we opened it, and then go into the side passage. In the passage under a window was an oak table.

"Up, up!"

On to the table he would leap and for the first time in about sixteen days, amid purrs, his harness would be taken off and hung behind the kitchen door.

Soon he would be going out and commencing his rounds. With some exaggeration we would say he was 'beating up the neighbourhood' but in reality he was back to his legitimate work after a well-earned holiday – keeping stray cats away, controlling the mouse and rabbit population, chasing away squirrels and generally living up to his reputation of being an excellent watch-cat. In that way it could be said that he paid for his bed and board, and thus earned his next trip to the mountains and next year's summer holiday by the sea and a rest from all those chores.

*Great Crested Grebes,
River Alde*